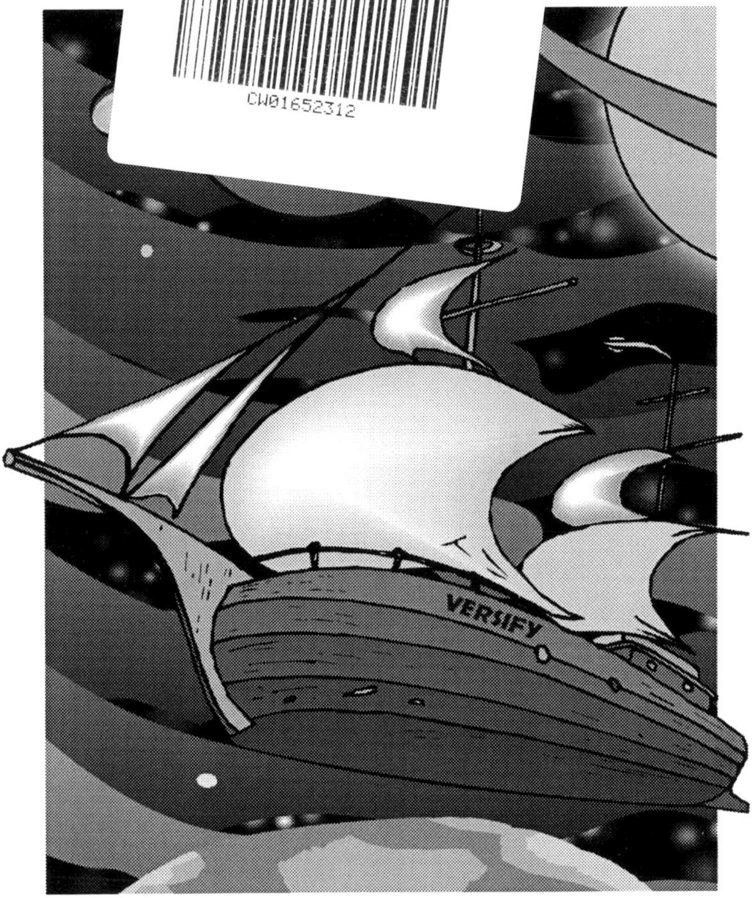

POETIC VOYAGES CAMBRIDGE

Edited by Lucy Jeacock

First published in Great Britain in 2001 by
YOUNG WRITERS
Remus House,
Coltsfoot Drive,
Peterborough, PE2 9JX
Telephone (01733) 890066

HB ISBN 0 75433 252 7
SB ISBN 0 75433 253 5

FOREWORD

Young Writers was established in 1991 with the aim to promote creative writing in children, to make reading and writing poetry fun.

This year once again, proved to be a tremendous success with over 88,000 entries received nationwide.

The Poetic Voyages competition has shown us the high standard of work and effort that children are capable of today. It is a reflection of the teaching skills in schools, the enthusiasm and creativity they have injected into their pupils shines clearly within this anthology.

The task of selecting poems was therefore a difficult one but nevertheless, an enjoyable experience. We hope you are as pleased with the final selection in *Poetic Voyages Cambridge* as we are.

CONTENTS

The Poems

DRAGON

Dragon! Wading through the lake,
Making all the tree trunks shake
Breathing fire, flying higher
The hungry giant awaits.
His massive claws, ready to scratch
Anything that comes to him for a match.
Slashing his tail viciously
Coming dangerously close to a tree.
His shiny scales glistening in the moonlight
Terrified villagers running away in fright.
Splattering blood all over the grass
They've attacked the dragon at last!

Rosie Brock (9)
Barton CE Primary School

It Has To Be In By Monday

It has to be in by Monday
and I haven't an idea in my head,
It has to be in by Monday
and I want to go to bed;
It has to be in by Monday
and my brain feels like mushy peas,
It has to be in by Monday
oh please, please, please;
It has to be in by Monday
and I don't know what to do,
It has to be in by Monday
Oh boo hoo, hoo, hoo.

James Gibbs (10)
Barton CE Primary School

On Sunday

On Sundays I go to see my dad,
I like it because I'm never sad,
He picks me up at quarter to ten
Then we go back to his den.
Tracey's there cooking food,
My sister's always in a mood.
The bacon's always under the grill
And when it's done I have my fill.
Or we have a salmon fish,
Which always is a tasty dish,
Then we go to the Red Bull,
Where we always play a game of football.
We go and see my nan,
Just because we know we can.
I always have a Sunday roast,
I usually also eat the most.
Then we have a lazy afternoon,
Because I know I go home soon.
When the day is done, I go home to see my mum,
My dad rings in the week,
Usually when it's off-peak.
I can't wait for Sunday to come again,
So my dad can pick me up at quarter to ten.

Tom Evemy (11)
Barton CE Primary School

THE FOOTBALL MATCH

I walked into a packed stadium,
To witness Huddersfield Town vs Crystal Palace.
Fans talking and laughing before the game,
The stadium announcer announcing the teams.
Huddersfield took the kick-off.
Both teams knocked the ball about,
Both cancelled each other out.
Then about fifteen minutes from time,
Huddersfield got a corner.
The ball came to Huddersfield's star player,
Bang, 1-0
Palace went from cheering happily to holding their heads.
It looked like another defeat for Palace when,
The ball came to Palace's star player from a cross whack,
1-1
Second half started square.
Palace youth ran into the box, foul! Penalty!
Oh no, he missed it.
A Palace striker rounded then he missed.
Then a Palace corner came to our player *Ppppplllleat* . . .
2-1, all over
Not bad for a defender!
Near the end, Huddersfield's fans had nearly all gone,
Palace fans cheered 'Cheerio, cheerio.'
Full time, 2-1 Palace,
Up the league we went.

Richard Gladders (9)
Barton CE Primary School

FIREWORKS

Sparkling through the November sky,
Whizzing round and round,
Flying and fizzing ever so high,
Making a really loud sound,
Splashing colours into the air,
Sizzling up and down,
Then disappearing like they were never there,
But never hitting the ground.

Daniel Chapman (11)
Barton CE Primary School

MONITOR, HARD DRIVE, ACTION

I am a computer
and that is very true
I have lots of functions
that really can help you

Browse the net
Play a game
Do your shopping
Book a plane

I know that people use me
almost every day
and if they didn't like me
they would just throw me away

Adults have to do their work
and children come to play
They sometimes do their homework
On a homework day

My owner is called Alex
and he is ten years old
I use Windows 2000
because that is what I'm told

I'm glad that I'm so useful
I'm glad that I'm so cool
I'm glad that Alex plays with me
when he comes home from school.

Alex Noble (10)
Barton CE Primary School

If I Were A Football . . .

If I were a football
Small and round
being kicked upon the ground
flying through the crimson skies
and landing on some Celtic guys.

If I were a football
Light and fast
being chipped and being passed
being smashed against the post
wishing I could burn like toast.

If I were a football
Easy to see
being hurt so easily
watching a very obvious hack
behind the referee's hunched back.

If I were a football
Old and brave
being beaten like a slave
crashing on a stadium top
knowing I was gonna pop
being kicked by a studded shoe
I think I'd be scared
don't you!

Andrew Richards (11)
Barton CE Primary School

Cats

Cats' dark blue eyes
creeping about the garden
calling birds
and mice as they play.

Jumping fences and climbing trees
running through the wet and slippery grass
catching each other's tails
as they pass.

Time for something to eat
miaowing and asking for
the teatime treats after
a full and satisfying
bowl of milk and meat.

They like to curl upon a mat
in front of a warm and glowing
fire and sleep quietly
until the morning dawn.

Kirsty Louise Badcock (10)
Barton CE Primary School

SPACE

S pace is massive
P eace and quiet
A universe full of stars
C ircular are the moon and Earth
E njoy space the way it is.

Lauren Victoria Martin (10)
Barton CE Primary School

My Miraculous Mind

My mind is a miraculous thing
It gives me ideas in a ping!
It memorises pictures totally the best
It always works, no time to rest
It acts like a cage, or a cardboard box
And my memories it carefully locks
It has so many sections, all different sizes
Each one is different, full of surprises
It fizzes and pops when you get too tired
Into your brain, it seems to get wired

My memory is always on
Telling me secret thoughts all day
It tells me not to do something naughty twice
Working, it always remembers
It will fill up all the nooks and crannies
Putting me in deep, deep thought

My memory is even better still
Making me remember how to use a grill
I still remember lots of friends
The long, long list probably never ends
Recalling millions and millions of faces
Like a camera filming races
The colours flashing through my brain
Like blue, red and purple rain
Thoughts whizzing from bit to bit
I hope that my brain will never quit

My memory is always on
Telling me secret thoughts all day
It tells me not to do something naughty twice
Working, it always remembers
It will fill up all the nooks and crannies
Putting me in deep, deep thought.

Hannah Nelms (9)
Barton CE Primary School

Cats Big And Small

Lions are very dangerous big cats!
They are big and fierce and everyone is afraid of them.
But my neighbour's cat is little and cute,
She's always kind except to the mice,
It killed two last night, but I still think she's nice.

Ian R Lewis (9)
Barton CE Primary School

THE EAGLE

The eagle soars from mountain to mountain
looking for his prey.
The eagle swoops from tree to tree
looking for its prey.

The eagle soars and spots his prey,
The eagle glides and stalks his prey,
The eagle zooms down to Earth
and catches his prey!

Chris Hardwick (9)
Barton CE Primary School

THE MACAW

I have been told
That once in flight
The majestic macaw
Is a dazzling sight.

As his wings unfold
And his talons withdraw
He flies over treetops
And the ground is no more.
He soars through the air
And lands on a branch
Then he begins his
Courtship dance.

Harry Finkel (11)
Barton CE Primary School

The Last Of England

In the raging sea, the waves crash on the cliffs,
The little boat rocks, one way then the other,
We don't know what is happening, but we're leaving England for good,
Our friends have gone to Australia, and we're going to join them
Whatever happens.
They say it's all bush and red sand.
How are we going to survive?
But it's too late to turn back now
As the last view disappears.
I look ahead, but there is nothing
For miles and miles and many more miles.
I see a storm and then big rocks.
For once in my life, I'm overcome by terror.
Water pouring in, I think we're going to drown!
What will happen next?

Alice Kay (9)
Bottisham Community Primary School

The Last Of England

Looking into the distance . . .
Seeing the last of my country,
England.
Tearfully, I look and say
'We will be safe,' I say to my baby.
We are going to Australia to get some food.
We have been chucked out of our house,
Because we are poor and people are invading our country.
We are moving for good.
There are bombs everywhere.
Sea rushing so fast past the boat.
So rough and waving like white horses jumping up and down.
We will be there soon.

Jessica Dobbyne (9)
Bottisham Community Primary School

VOYAGE TO CYBERSPACE

5, 4, 3, 2, 1
Up we go, the rocket's gone
We're going to cyberspace
Going at a speedy pace
It's still very far
Until we reach the famous star

Look, there's the cheesy moon
It's not cheese like in a cartoon.

Oh! Look! There's an alien!
It's green and slimy
Big, not tiny
It's spooky and scary
(Not like a fairy)

We've landed in cyberspace
Silver and futuristic.
So now it's
Time for a
Big bye, bye.

Natashja Kasianczuk (8)
Bottisham Community Primary School

THE PLANE

The plane flew high
Up into the sky
My mum was bored
My sister snored
The lady came
As I was playing a game
We all felt fine
My mum and dad had wine.

Alice Burton (8)
Bottisham Community Primary School

VOYAGE AT SEA

We set sail on the wavy deep blue sea,
The wind lapped the sails and we raced along.
When night fell there was a storm,
The rain was falling like metal pellets,
The clouds covered all the bright shining stars,
So we couldn't see which way to navigate.
The lightning struck down like a razor-sharp knife,
The thunder bellowed like a volcano,
But somehow we slept.
When morning came it was as calm as icing on a cake,
The sun's heat made us more cheerful.
Then we saw land on the horizon,
It was such a terrific moment when the wind blew us along.
Finally we were safe on dry land.

Josie Urquhart (7)
Bottisham Community Primary School

A Sea Serpent

I saw a sea serpent at sea
And it bit a hole in me.
I went to see a doctor and he said to me
'I can't do any thing, you see.
Go back to the sea and sail along,
With your friendly pirates and go back
To your voyages with me.'

Laura Clarke (7)
Bottisham Community Primary School

Space Voyage

Before I can go to space
I have to tie up my lace
I get into the rocket and say 'One, two, three'
I scratch my knee
Three, two, one. Blast off!

I see Mars
I see the stars
It's high up here
Space must be near
Space, here I come!

It's amazing on the moon
I'll have to go home soon
I won't want to go
But I'll go in one big blow
Space is great!

Sophie Darling (9)
Bottisham Community Primary School

THE SPACESHIP

The spaceship goes up into the sky,
It zooms and zooms up ever so high,
In your spacesuit so you can breathe,
We turn a switch so we can leave,

Higher and higher, I feel quite sick,
At least I can talk to the captain called Nick,
I'm going to lie down because I'm going to die,
I won't get to sleep, because we're up so high.

Lucy Astill (7)
Bottisham Community Primary School

THE UNICORN

The amazing unicorn
Twisting and twirling
Its golden wings
fluttering and flapping.

The amazing unicorn
Gliding through the sky
So magic, so wonderful
Its fascinating horn
Silver as a star
It flies back up to the flossy clouds.

Lauren Grace Wilson (8)
Bottisham Community Primary School

Trains

I like riding on trains
TGVs are fast
The Union Pacific
its power is vast.

Carting goods across America
it doesn't stop at night
the TGV goes in the Eurotunnel
it's dark, it gives me a fright.

Matthew James Burns (9)
Bottisham Community Primary School

If You Want To See A Baby Dolphin

If you want to see a baby dolphin
You must go down to the deepest
Bluest water
I know a baby dolphin who's living there
She's kind, she's new and she's blue.

Yes, if you really want to see a baby dolphin
You must go down to the deepest
Bluest water
Go down quietly and say
'Baby dolphin
Baby dolphin
I've got some fish for you
Come and get it
Come and get it
And then I will love you.'

Lorna Glennie (9)
Bottisham Community Primary School

MY DAD'S CAR

My dad's car is old,
My dad is never selling it,
It's bright red, like a ladybird,
It has a black hood that folds back,
And I love riding in it.
I put my arm over the side
And my hair blows all over the place.
When we go to the car show
Me and Mike and his girlfriend go round the ring.
I like to go to the car show,
My dad helps me clean and polish it,
It sparkles when it has been cleaned.
I love my dad and his car.

Katie Gaskin (7)
Bottisham Community Primary School

It's Snowing

The snow is falling very fast
Down from the sky today.
It looks so soft and shiny
I want to go outside and play.

Aaron Sutherland (7)
Bottisham Community Primary School

The Penguin

The penguin waddles home,
It's dark and gloomy,
The sun has gone down.
He hears his little baby penguin call,
His daddy waddles up to him
And gives him a hug.
He goes and sees his wife
And then they sleep soundly.

Lucy Lamport (8)
Bottisham Community Primary School

AUTUMN

Crispy, golden, ever-falling leaves,
Rustle softly in the autumn breeze,
All of the colours, yellow, brown and red,
Leave the tree branches, making them look dead,
The days are getting cold,
The nights are growing old,
While the leaves are gently turning,
You watch the blazing bonfire burning,
Then the dancing hot flames,
Fade as the bonfire tames,
And it's lonely once more,
As you crunch the twigs on the floor,
The wind blows and blows,
As it nips at your toes,
It's time to wrap up warm,
Because summer has gone.

Ellie Farrington (8)
Bottisham Community Primary School

HOLIDAY BLUES

Decision has been made
Destination chosen
Date has been set
A holiday; hip, hip, hooray!

The morning awakes
The excitement escalates
The last list boxes are ticked.

Doors are locked
Escalators riding
It's a nice lady
'Have you flown before?'

A roar, a drink, a kick
I'm seeing clouds go by
Book in hand, sleep in mind
I'm tired now
I think I will sleep because when I wake
I will be on a sandy beach.

Natasha McKitterick (8)
Bottisham Community Primary School

STORM

Silver sparkles, lightning hits the waves,
Torpedoes turn the sea round and round.
Octopuses wiggle on the sand as they relax.
Round and round the sea turns.
Man eating fish, fish eating jelly fish.

Victoria Rice (8)
Bottisham Community Primary School

Rocket Balloon

I'm going to the moon
On a rocket balloon
I'm going to take a blanket
Some cherries and apple pie
For if I don't, I'm sure to die -
I'll go inside a box
Attached to the balloon
So if I stay very calm
I'm sure to reach the moon,
I've taken some oxygen in a pump
It looks as though I've got a lump
On top of my rocket balloon.

Sofia Janjua (8)
Bottisham Community Primary School

THE AMAZING SUNSET

The sun is like a golden eagle,
That shines in the growing dark,
And glimmering on the horizon,
It glows among the moon and stars,
The trees are growing longer,
By the shadows of good or bad,
The clouds are getting pink and fluffy,
So are the apples and pears,
The sun has gone,
The night is starting once more.

Jorge Monteiro (10)
Bottisham Community Primary School

THE BEACH

The beach has beautiful sand,
The singers sing in a band,
The coconuts clapping together,
Where they all go nobody knows,
The sun is rising, now it's morning,
Porridge for breakfast,
Oh that's boring!

Elissa Spaxman (9)
Bottisham Community Primary School

SUNSET ISLAND

The warm sun slowly sets,
The sea is calm and gentle,
It softly laps the lonely shore,
On the peaceful, deserted island,
Its pure white sands sparkle,
And its palm trees silent and still,
The sound of the gentle waves
Is all that can be heard.

Amy Farrington (11)
Bottisham Community Primary School

The Greyest Of Skies

The greyest of skies,
Hangs over the sea,
The spray and the foam,
Fly over the boat.

The wind is a-howling,
And driving the seagulls,
But the whale is still calm,
As it waits underwater,
Till the storm dies down again.

Sally Pearl (10)
Bottisham Community Primary School

SUNSET

The sunset's gleaming in the sky
Casting red, orange and yellow shadows
It's starting to get darker and quieter
Suddenly everything is silent.

Julia Saville (9)
Bottisham Community Primary School

SUNSET

The sun was lying quietly in the sky,
as the colours in my mind went by,
purple, orange, yellow, red,
pink, blue in my head.
The sunset in the sky was still,
just like the water beyond the hill.

Libby Tennant (9)
Bottisham Community Primary School

The City Above

The city above is very quiet,
the sun is setting in the night sky.
The city slam has finished,
the sun is nearly below the crust.
Everybody is fast asleep,
soon that will be true for me.
As the night sky goes by,
the moon is rising to guard the night sky.

Joshua George (10)
Bottisham Community Primary School

The Lonely Palm Tree

It stands in the middle of the beach,
And watches the sun go down,
Everybody's gone home now,
The murmur travels through the town.

Sophie Wood (9)
Bottisham Community Primary School

THE STORM

The waves crashed against the pointed rocks,
The rain came tumbling down,
No birds in the sky or people on the ground.
Just the lightning bolts coming down.

The sky was a dull grey,
The sea a dark blue.
The sun was hiding behind the clouds,
Only just peeping through.

Jemma Mynott (11)
Bottisham Community Primary School

The Sunset

The sun shines on the horizon,
It gleams over the sea,
The sun shines on the horizon,
And it completely amazes me.

Joshua Pencheon (10)
Bottisham Community Primary School

The Sea

The waves are washing
onto the sand

Which looks to me like a
long yellow band.

The wind blows and
rustles the grass

And the foam on the sea
goes floating past.

Claire Morley (10)
Bottisham Community Primary School

The Sunset

The sunset shines in the gleaming sky
It is very pretty as it travels by
The palm trees whistle and shake in the wind
The coconuts fall off and hit the ground
Making a soft and gentle sound
The sand is very hot, very dry
As it glitters under the moonlight sky.

Ben Stopher (10)
Bottisham Community Primary School

SUNSET OVER A DESERT ISLAND

The sun is gleaming in
the sky,
Over the desert
Island,
It shines from above as
The wind blows by,
And all is peace
And quiet.

The leaves of the palm trees
Blow around,
As the sun finally sets in
The sky,
You can hear the sound of coconuts
Fall to the ground,
As the sun
Passes by.

Michelle Hall (11)
Bottisham Community Primary School

SUNSET

When I look at the sun on the horizon,
I think a new world has begun,
With all the colours under the sun.
It's almost as if God has got a paintbrush
And painted the sky so many different colours.
It's unbelievably pretty.

Hannah Linsey (9)
Bottisham Community Primary School

The Beach

The sea is calm and the sun shines bright,
The sand burns anything, so you're in the chair
with the umbrella, exhausted. Seagulls fly above,
to their nests on cliffs up high, with a screech
and a squeal. They rest as the sun goes down.
I watch the soft wind blow the sand.

Zahra Al-Masoud (9)
Bottisham Community Primary School

THE WAR

Army on standby
Navy on the sea
The air raid siren goes
The army fights back.

Smoke and flames pour out
Germans dropping bombs
Bangs and screams.

It was so loud,
The world could
Hear it all!

James Good (8)
Bottisham Community Primary School

FROZEN LIZARD

I'm a lonely lizard
Who's stuck in a blizzard
Who's going to save me like a wizard?

My favourite dish
Searching for leftovers, bones of fish!
My favourite wish -
Get me out of this!

Nils De Geer Wikner (8)
Bottisham Community Primary School

A Racing Car

Racing round the wiggly track
Going at the speed of light

Here comes the racing car
I'm winning, I'm winning

But no
Quickly, quickly, jack up the car
Quickly, quickly change the tyre
Off we roar
I'm winning, I'm winning
I've won!

Gabriel Clarke (7)
Bottisham Community Primary School

SALAMANDERS

The legend says
They walk through fire,
They do it for days and days
I know something they really admire.

They eat trays of cold ice cream!
I know it sounds so silly,
It is every salamander's dream,
They like things that are chilly!

Not curry, not meat,
They want something cold to eat!

Sam Bristow (9)
Bottisham Community Primary School

Animals In Winter

What's that noise thumping in my ears,
I think it's Whinny winter rabbit,
Oh! Look, Percy polar bear is roaring his head off,
Harry hound pulling a sledge,
Whistling Rocket robin is blasting off to space,
Pingo penguin flying in the sea,
Harvey hedgehog hibernating.

People wrapping up warm,
People wearing woolly jumpers,
People drinking hot chocolate,
People eating toast as hot as an oven!

So roll on summer.

Joseph Millard (8)
Bottisham Community Primary School

THE NOT SO GOOD HOLIDAY

Here I am in Jamaica
My husband is coming soon, not later
Under the mango tree I lie
Staring up at the light blue sky
A mango drops upon my head
But I don't want to spend my holiday in bed!

So out surfing I go
Then I spot my husband Jo
We swim with the dolphins together
We could swim and swim and swim forever.

Then I spot my dreaded mother and hide
Under the dock for cover
Suddenly she finds us hiding
Now I know she won't take us gliding!

Today we will have to pack our suitcase
But I was planning to buy a new boot lace!

Now we're on the plane to take us home
Now I wish we had come alone!

Thea Frances Reeves (8)
Bottisham Community Primary School

The Sea Horse

A magical sparkling sea horse
Gallops along the seabed
Covered in wonderful colours
Like beautiful gold and red.

Its hooves give off light
And its mane and tail
Cover its face
Like a golden veil.

Emma Pencheon (8)
Bottisham Community Primary School

Sky Of Colours

The dark, starry sky of night,
Is turning into morning light,
No sun or clouds yet arise,
But colours fill the morning skies,
A lonely palm tree stands and stands,
Upon an island's golden sands.

Ashleigh Clowes (11)
Bottisham Community Primary School

Sunset On Gracy Island

The stripes of colour fill the sky,
The island black against the light,
A few black-headed gulls fly by,
As day turns to night.

The palm trees look like giant hands,
With fingers stretching uppermost,
Piercing through the coloured bands,
As the sun sets at the coast.

Oliver Pimley (9)
Bottisham Community Primary School

Sunset

The sun is setting in the sky,
The clouds all fluffy drifting by,
While all the little bats come out,
I will watch them flying about.

So when the sun has set completely,
The moon shines intensely
Another day has passed
With me watching the sunset while it lasts.

Katrin Hulme (10)
Bottisham Community Primary School

SUNSET BEACH

Sun setting warm and bright,
All is peaceful, calm and light,
The sea is lapping against the shore,
Birds sing their song once more,
The leaning palm tree still stands,
With the wind blowing against the sand.

Shona Fordham (10)
Bottisham Community Primary School

The Sea

The sun beams to your eyes,
The sea smashes onto a rock,
The trees give you shade,
The birds sing a lullaby.

The sun is setting in the sky,
The sea is taking the sun's image,
The birds are going to bed,
The water's changing colour.

Simon Cooper (10)
Bottisham Community Primary School

DEEP BLUE SEA

I'm sitting on the island
Looking at the sea,
The sun has set, it's getting dark,
The fish are jumping up and down.
The ships are sailing far, far away.
I'm settling down on the sand,
I close my eyes and wonder
Why I am here,
It's time to say goodbye.

Mark Bruno (10)
Bottisham Community Primary School

ISOLATION

Sitting on the sand
The wind whistling through my hair,
Isolation.
The waves lap the shore
As I walk along the sand
Isolation.
I watch the sunset in the sky
While sitting among the palm trees,
Isolation.

Lizzie Turner (9)
Bottisham Community Primary School

The Sunset Poem

Wind is blowing through my hair,
As I sit in my deck chair,
Seagulls fly by,
As I look up in the sky,
Quiet as can be,
Sitting under a palm tree.
I imagine that I'm at home,
While I'm looking at the sea's foam,
The sun is setting in the sky,
My day has quietly passed by.

Laura Durrant (10)
Bottisham Community Primary School

GOLD

Gold is the colour of victory standing proudly
All around the world,
Gold is also the colour of an Olympic medal,
Gold is the great kings protected crown,
Gold is the golden boot, a greatly talented footballer,
Gold is the colour of the sun gleaming on us,
Gold is the great treasure buried underground,
Gold is the colour of a hard golden tooth,
Crunching round sweetcorn.

Jamie Nightingale (9)
Bottisham Community Primary School

Black

Black is the darkest of nights,
Black is the cloak that washes over the evening,
Swallowing it up like a worm hole,
Black is the shadow that creeps along beside you,
Until it slowly disappears into darkness,
Eaten by the evening,
The night sky is black as ebony,
Until the sun decides to wake
At last the black fades away.

Denise Barry (10)
Bottisham Community Primary School

WHITE

White is the colour of the froth on my hot chocolate,
White is the mist that wraps around towns,
Losing them to the intense white,
White hot embers on a dying bonfire,
After the blazing inferno has died away,
White wax from a candle racing in drops,
To the base to gather in a shapeless blob,
White chalk on an ebony, black, blackboard,
White marks, constructing words and numbers,
White is nothing,
Blank,
Empty,
Waiting to be coloured by the busy world.

Tom Ward (11)
Bottisham Community Primary School

Blue

Blue is the colour of sea, sky and river,
It is the colour of Neptune, the planet of God,
Water is blue running through the tap,
A Pepsi can is red and blue,
My jumper is blue,
As blue as the sky,
Blue, blue, blue.

Roger Smith (9)
Bottisham Community Primary School

Red, Orange, Green

Red is the colour of scented roses,
Red is the colour of shining lips,
Red is the colour of bright blood.

Green is the colour of long grass,
Green is the colour of apple trees,
Green is the colour of newborn leaves.

Orange is the colour of sweet mandarins,
Orange is the colour of juicy passion fruit,
Orange is the colour of ripe peaches.

Red, orange and green are
The colours of traffic lights.

Hannah Al-Masoud (10)
Bottisham Community Primary School

Black

Slugs are ugly bugs that are black
You don't want to find them crawling
Up your back.
Black are spiders who hide in places
Most unexpected.
Black is the colour
Of the blackboard
That gives life to an awaiting
White piece of chalk.
Black is the colour of ink
Pressing down on the paper,
Black is the colour that gives
Us charcoal and
Makes us have the fun of
Smudging our work.
Black is the colour of the universe
That is amazingly enormous,
Too big to believe.
So black is black is black,
What is black?

James Mynott (9)
Bottisham Community Primary School

Blue

Blue is the roaring, crashing sea,
Blue is an icicle hanging down,
Blue is a tiny raindrop,
Blue is frozen ice,
Blue is the feel of chattering teeth,
Blue is the sky on a scorching
Summer day that goes on for
Miles and never ends.
Blue is like a glistening pool
That shimmers in the moonlight,
Blue is thundering rain that
Pours down day and night.

Yasmin Alderson (10)
Bottisham Community Primary School

RED

Red are the round berries birds
Pick off the green thorny bush,
As Valentine hearts fall down,
Slowly . . . softly,

Red is the colour
Your eyes change to at your
Dad's bad attempt to take a photo.

Red is the colour of the bold
Fire lit in front of you,
As your face turns crimson hot.

Red is the pale colour of roses
Standing in line after line
After line after line . . .

Vicki Hodgson (9)
Bottisham Community Primary School

ORANGE

An orange is juicy and dribbly
Under its orange coat of skin,
An exciting bright burning light
Wondering what's going to happen.
A sparkling wet scaled skin goldfish.
Orange is the colour of a burning fire,
Have you got it yet?
Orange is my favourite colour.

Rory McCabe (9)
Bottisham Community Primary School

RED

Red is the sign of oozing blood,
Red is the colour of a stop signal,
Roaring rocket red bursting off to space.

Blue is the colour of the sky in summer,
Blue is the sign of an angel's personality,
Blue is the pencil case sitting on my desk.

White is the smoke of an angry ghost,
White is the shiny paper on my desk,
Red and blue stripes.

White stars.

Come together to make the USA flag.

Stephen Titchmarsh (10)
Bottisham Community Primary School

FIGHT FOR REIGN OF THE SKY

Orange is the centrepiece of the early evening sky,
Glowing in its glory, before the world's eyes.
Suddenly the real night comes
Ebony darkness dashes across the vivid flames,
Like a candle, just a flicker and the party dies.
The jet black daggers pierce the skin of the flamboyant inferno,
'It bleeds, it bleeds' echoes the burning voices.
The maroon liquid trickles down to the silhouetted horizon
The darkness bellowed with laughter
The cacophony rang like bells throughout the sky,
A terracotta mist sinks down behind the city
Sobbing heavily,
A shrieking whine rang out
The night had won.

Jonathan Harker (11)
Bottisham Community Primary School

Red

Red as the sunset when you know it's
Going to be a pleasant tomorrow.
Red as your trousers when you're going
To a disco.
Red like an angry face on your teacher
Waiting to tell you off.
Red as a smooth rose petal in your garden.
Redder than an extremely scary drop slide
In the park.
Redder than my every day jumper, faded by
The washing machine.

Beth Greenall (9)
Bottisham Community Primary School

My Special Rainbow

Brown is the colour of rocks on the shore,
Brown is the colour of the wood in the fire,
Brown is the colour of a desert as the sun sets,
Brown is dirty.

Blue is the colour of the sky in the inferno of summer,
Blue is the tiny bit of flame in the middle of your fire,
Blue will be the last sight before you perish to another world,
Blue is icy and cold.

Yellow is the colour of the round ball of flaming fire, the sun,
Yellow is a happy colour,
Yellow can be the colour of a thorny bush in winter,
Yellow reaches out like a bright light to you.

Joshua Hatley (11)
Bottisham Community Primary School

YELLOW

Sun and stars, hot, bright, firey, flames,
Burning out, crumbly wheat, all flaky,
Dying plants, sad and weeping.

Demon eyes looking down all evil,
Flowers so beautiful, dandelions, daffodils,
Sand running through my feet
Carried by the lapping waves.

Birds waking up in the summer sun,
Hay being eaten in the bright light,
As we eat potatoes while drinking juice,
The morning sky has a hint of yellow.

Yellow is the colour of life.

Sophie Millard (9)
Bottisham Community Primary School

Gold And Orange

Gold and orange looking like flickering flames in
The darkness jerking around vigorously like an angry
Demon on the prowl. Gold and orange like a full field of
Corn ready to be harvested with pale brown mice
Running around.
Birds picking the squelching ones.
Birds stuffing their bills full of juicy berries
Rapidly, greedy, stuffed juice dropping
From their golden beaks.

Rebecca Aldrich (10)
Bottisham Community Primary School

RED

Red is the burning fire glowing in the darkness.
Red berries falling down to the long, wavy grass
Where birds are feasting.
The rosy love hearts lying on the ground.
My red embarrassed face is a flaming ball of fire sizzling.
The garnet roses sway from side to side
In cold winds.
Red is bright,
Bold,
Angry,
The squirts of runny, red, blood dripping from your body,
The red fire burns down.

Poppy Smith (10)
Bottisham Community Primary School

Fiver

Fiver is a bunny
He has a soft white coat
He's as white as snow
And as soft as velvet.
He has long loopy ears,
He has a little tail like a fluffy
White cloud,
He has big back feet
And a tiny pink nose.
He's as white as a clean page,
Waiting to be written on,
Fiver is a flash of white rushing by,
He's like a snowball,
Being hurled around his
Own tiny world.
Fiver is a bunny.

Emma Whitehead (9)
Bottisham Community Primary School

White

White is the colour of a clean new page
And ice on a wet road,
White is the whine of a lonely child,
White is the powder from a well greased ski,
Sidelines on a football pitch
And the colour from a peeling silver birch tree,
White is also the colour of a cold icy sky,
White is the colour that shines in our hearts.

Nicola Bloxham (11)
Bottisham Community Primary School

Red

Blood is the colour of red,
The wicked devil in scary hell,
The fast fire engines whizz past,
The blazing fire in the cosy living room,
The explosions in the dreaded war,
Children come to school with their bright red jumpers,
The shiny red buses wait and wait,
You get mad when your face turns red,
The cone shaped fire extinguisher waiting to be used,
Red is inside you,
Yes you!

Daniel Seakins (10)
Bottisham Community Primary School

Green

Green is the colour of the grass that sways in the wind,
Green is the colour of the rustling leaves,
It can be a file full of secret documents,
Green is the colour of a bright, bold school chair,
A patch of mould on a crusty piece of bread,
Green is the colour of a bright green football pitch,
Just ready to be ran on by football players.
An iguana scrambling through the giant forest,
Green is a stalk of a growing plant
And as the sun sets green disappears
Over the horizon.

Luke Nudds (10)
Bottisham Community Primary School

POOL BLUE

Pool blue skies over the summer fields,
Field mice rushing around for food,
Putting the paddling pool out to keep cool,
Listening to music in a land of blue dolphins,
Swimming across the duvet covers,
Writing a story in your best blue folder,
With your best blue pen,
Taking it to school the next day for choir
With your best song in it.

That is why my favourite colour is . . .
Pool Blue!

Stefanie Raw (9)
Bottisham Community Primary School

GREEN

A great bright blanket spread across the
World swaying dramatically.
When the wild wind of the west blows fiercely.

Green are the apples, big, ripe and juicy,
Ready to be picked, struggling to break
From brown branches on a twisted, spiky tree.

Nothing greater than the mighty green
Crocodile with greedy snapping jaws.

Tony Lynam (9)
Bottisham Community Primary School

My Mum

Mum has got blonde hair,
She is really nice,
She cooks me scrambled eggs
And always makes my bed.

The only thing is
She wears the strangest clothes,
Purple trousers, bright green tops,
Pink socks with polka dots,
A baseball cap in brilliant blue
And none of it is new!
She really does belong in a zoo!

Louise Whitt (8)
Caldecote Primary School

Fife

There was a dog called Fife,
Who ate his dinner with a knife.
The dog had a very contented life,
Except that he wanted a wife.

Fife went to the park,
When it was really dark,
He met a dog called Joy
Who turned out to be a boy!

Fife went off to sea,
In a boat made of tea.
He could not find a wife,
But that's life!

Charlotte Burgess (7)
Caldecote Primary School

THE WIZARD

Wise, wicked wizard,
Making wishes all day long,
Waving his wizardly, wicked wand,
All the way, every day.

While he does his wicked deeds,
He waves his hand again,
His hand waves in a wizardly way.
Suddenly his hand turns around and says
'Wicked wizard go away!'

Bethany Purser (8)
Caldecote Primary School

THE BROWN HORSE

The brown horse sat in the green, green grass,
When he saw something in the shed.
He galloped off to have a look
When he got there, he found it was a bear,
Sitting in a chair.

David Nash (8)
Caldecote Primary School

SCHOOL

The bell goes at nine o'clock,
Into school we go,
Teacher calls the register,
We put our lunch away.

We do our spellings quickly,
We have to get them correct,
Then it's maths and literacy,
It's always hard - you bet!

Lunchtimes we eat our dinner
And out to play we go,
Come back in for art and games
It's always fun you know.

Home time comes round quickly,
It's time to say goodbye,
I can't wait till tomorrow
Geography, science and fun!

Jay Phillips (7)
Caldecote Primary School

THE COW

The brown, brown cow
Ate the green, green grass,
When the orange sun
Caused her to run
And take cover
Under the old, oak tree.

Then the farmer came
And milked her again
Then he made some cheese
Which made him pleased,
With the brown, brown cow
Who ate the green, green grass.

Liam Johnson (7)
Caldecote Primary School

Tears Of War

The ground was shaking as bomb V2 exploded,
A cloud of thick black smoke surrounded the city.
People were falling onto the floor like tigers,
Caught in a hunter's trap.

A surge of unhappiness slithered down my spin,
I felt so sorry for the soldiers' families . . .
Little did they know,
That . . . their brother may be lying in those muddy trenches or
Perhaps lying in a hospital bed.
Moaning and missing their family dreadfully.

I did not know it but the sound of the siren buzzing in my ears . . . and

People crying in the thick black smoke.
The thought of people lying in the trenches filled my eyes with salty
Crystal clear tears.
They ran down my pink cheeks onto the bomb shelter floor.
There they lay, rippling because of the aeroplanes soaring over my
head.

Will war ever end?
The soldiers in heaven seemed to say as my tears drifted away.

Katie Speed (9)
Caldecote Primary School

FOOTBALL CRAZY

I'm football crazy
I'm football mad
I love football
Just like my dad.

My dad likes Liverpool
I like Man U
I like Caldecote Crusaders
How about you?

I love football
I play three times a week
I try and do great headers
But sometimes it stings my cheek.

I play in the sun
I play in the rain
I love to be muddy
'Cause, I'm totally insane.

We won on Tuesday
It was great fun since
Our coach is a great lady
Her name is Mrs Quince.

Our school team plays on Wednesdays
It's great fun
Rolling in the mud
Just upsets our mum.

She has to do our washing
She really gets fed up
But what does she expect
If we're gonna win the cup.

So come on all and cheer us
Let's give it our best
We're Caldecote Crusaders
Forget all the rest.

So cheer us all through the wind and rain,
'Cause Caldecote Crusaders is our name.

Yeah!

Kris Phillips (10)
Caldecote Primary School

Expiration

Expiration be not a proud sight:
The dying on the street be not glory when decayed.
These dying people facing their plight,
Laid in the churchyard dark, end our fight.
The slowing heartbeat of those people, doth start to fade.
In the midst of the darkness the dead will reign,
They all travel on the dark and dead train.
On their own dead path, they doth walk.
The decrepit bodies, they doth still lie,
All these sorry people so soon will die.
Efforts to try and save them have been in vain,
The devil, prey he does stalk!
This poem be not for the faint hearted.

Jonathan Bentley-Smith (10) & Matthew Large
Caldecote Primary School

School

School can be good, school can be bad,
You have to go so don't be sad!

School can be cool, school can be fun,
You have to go if you don't want to be dumb!

School makes you clever, school makes you bright,
You have to go so don't pick a fight!

These are the things that my mum says
But I wish I was back in bed.
But I'm here in the classroom
Doing all the work,
I've got to do it 'cause I'm not a jerk!

Samantha Nash (10)
Caldecote Primary School

THE NIGHTMARE

He stood hauntingly,
I felt fear sweep over me.
His hands were covered in blue cracks,
Which smelt like a dead body.
His face, pale green, a blue tongue,
Hanging over his shoulder.
His teeth, nothing like I had ever seen before,
The front teeth, fangs, deep, black fangs
And worst of all the skull upon his chest!

Christopher Bentley-Smith (10)
Caldecote Primary School

TWICKENHAM

Playing for your country,
Playing with the best,
Playing the mighty Allblacks,
Better than the rest.
Playing at Franklin's Gardens,
Playing at Lansdown Road,
The best is the place we beat,
The Irish.
You know where it is,
Just take a left turn on the A316
It's Twickenham!
You know the team!
So come on down and cheer
England on and have some fun!
End of the day (What a day)
See you tomorrow.

Tommy Marr (10)
Caldecote Primary School

The Kitten And The Golden Leaves

The kitten sat upon the wall
And watched the garden's gold leaves fall.
Such wonder for the tiny cat,
So on the wall, she stayed and sat.
She licked her paws as quiet as ever,
The little pussy near the heather.
First one leaf and then another,
Now its sister, now its brother.
She starts to purr as she caught a leaf,
Her friend forever, in its belief,
It's autumn!

Katie Stoehr (10)
Caldecote Primary School

Stupid Cupid

There is a boy in our class called Cupid,
But everyone calls him Stupid,
When he does his work,
He chews the corner of his shirt,
So everyone calls him Stupid.

He was standing in the playground one day,
What he was doing, I can't say,
Another boy came along,
He said 'What is two times one?'
He answered 'Oh I don't know,
Fifty one, surely no,'
So all of us, everyone,
Called him Stupid.

His teacher said to him one day,
'If you know what's two times two, please say'
And then she said 'goodbye, good day,'
Then we all, all of us, we all called him stupid.

He came to school, looking glum,
In his eyes there was no sun.

We said to him 'Where is the sun?'
He said, 'I have no time to say,
My families dead and have to go away.'
Then all of us, everyone said
'Sorry'
Then turned away,
Perhaps he wasn't stupid,
Just very, very sad.

Holly Pearce (10)
Caldecote Primary School

A New School

What I want in my new school!
I would like a swimming pool,
For us to learn to swim.

A room for people who feel unwell
A nicer class and a new hall
Where we can exercise.

Come on builders, hurry up
Mix that cement and build those walls,
Hurry up and improve our school.

Amy Sandercock (9)
Caldecote Primary School

Football Match

The roar of the crowd like a huge lion.
The sun as bright as its own reflection on metal.
Out we strode onto the grass, everything was brilliant
In the Nou Camp.

Kick off, go! The ball speeds around the pitch.
No ditch, no concrete but perfect grass,
The real thing.
Speeding to goal, what a chance!
Goal! Joy unrivalled, the fans' cheering louder than ever.

Sweat, hot, both sides hot, sweaty, tired
Yet we still continue.
Not long till the break,
Just as well, exhaustion creeps in,
As unobtrusively as a lava flow.

Back out, the crowd's roar almost deafening - here we go!
Towards the goal we sprint, trying to score number two,
They've got it, phew we've got it back.
Hooray - goal two!

Match ending soon, again heat is not pleasure, it is pain,
We're gonna win,
'Cause it's two-nil, some faces are smiling,
Some faces are down, just like a picture,
Peep, peep, peep, the match is over.

It's all in the game . . . of football.

Richard Claridge (11)
Caldecote Primary School

AUTUMN BREEZE TO WINTER

Everything shines like the autumn jewelled grass,
Glinting like silver as the pupils change class!

The fresh breeze is cool you can tell autumn's coming,
Your fingers feel cool and begin to start numbing!

Bells of the new season tell us the reason why
Autumn is coming and our fingers are numbing!

Crunch, crunch, snap, snap, go the leaches at our feet,
The colours of autumn are brilliantly neat!

The Christmas tree's up, now the decorations,
Invite the friends and all the relations.
Open the presents, hip hip hooray,
Xmas is now so they all say!

The autumn trees rattle as the twigs battle,
Swish, swish goes the wind.
It is winter and as the juicy turkey bones are binned,
A New Year begins!

Esme Dora Banks Marr (9)
Caldecote Primary School

DARKNESS

Black darkness,
Lost the light,
On top of me.
On to me comes darkness,
Dead black night,
I seek the light, I see the dark.
I see the shadow of, I don't know what,
My heart pumps,
Blood turns black,
A shadow of darkness runs through my head,
At last I sleep.

Tania Saad Malik (10)
Caldecote Primary School

Ash And I

As I carefully mount, whispering reassuring
Words into his ears,
My leg swings over and my foot slips into the
Metal stirrups below me.

I kick him a little until he moves,
Moving slowly towards the ring.
Here we go into a march, marching
Along like soldiers in a war.

We come to a halt,
I open the gate quite slowly and steadily and
Walk through, shutting it behind us.
We march around the ring only once,
Just Ash and I.

The feeling was incredible just being there with him,
It was almost just like our minds were joined as one.

I decided to try a little trot before an eerie jump.
Giving him a whip and a kick telling him to go
Into working trot, obeyingly we went round the
Ring bouncing around, nudging him along the way
In sitting through to rising trot.

Once I finished, I lined us up for a jump,
A little bit taller than my knee height.
I started to trot and in my mind I saw myself
Lying on the ground all muddy and bruised,
Ash cantering off.

We were nearly at the jump, heart pounding
I folded and prayed.

We had cleared it, the judges raised signs reading 9's and 10's.
I took my hat off and said thank you to the judges and to Ash.

When we got to the dry and warm stable,
I gave him a massive hug for he had made me proud.

The future was very promising, we were one,
Just Ash and I.

Amy Hills (11)
Caldecote Primary School

My New School

Car park for the cars,
Art room for painting,
Library for us to read in
And a hall for us to sing in,
A science room to do
Experiments that we like best.

Football pitch for us to run around on,
Netball court to play on,
Equipment for the young ones,
Our playground is just the best.

Maths room for maths,
English room for English,
Our school is the best.
You will be impressed.

Ryan Cullingford & Lewis Newton (9)
Caldecote Primary School

FREE COUNTRY

If you live in a real free country,
Then you would see,
Fields, acres of fields,
Birds that fly free,
A stream that is fresh,
That is flowing, still going.
With all kinds of wildlife, roaming around.

Where I can have fun in the sun, on windy days
And in the rain,
Then maybe get on a saddled horse raring to go,
Off we go! Galloping round the field.
Where all people are free, in peace, with life.

That is my dream of a free country,
My free world.
But I know the world is changing
And my dream might be ending.

Emma Bicknell (11)
Caldecote Primary School

EIGHT HUNDRED AND FIFTY

Travelling along at eight hundred and fifty,
This train is really quite nifty.
Passing sheep in the fields that go by,
Travelling along at eight hundred and fifty.

I hear the call of the birds in the sky
That sing their song so fine.
Travelling along at eight hundred and fifty,
What's that I see? A tunnel up ahead with
Its walls, an almighty bright red.
Slowing down for a red light . . . travelling
Along at six hundred and sixty.

We are off again to the next stop
Gathering up passengers ready or not.
Travelling along at eight hundred and fifty,
This train is really quite nifty.

I see walkers on the verge, walking along
Disturbing the grass, so brave and tough.
They stride along just like me on a single line,
Lucky for us we're in this train not having to
Take all that pressure and pain.
Travelling along at eight hundred and fifty.

Getting bothered and hot, I want to go home to my lot,
Goodbye and good luck . . . getting slower and slower and slower.
Once this train was really quite nifty.
Travelling along at eight hundred and fifty.

Edward Waters & Jonathan Hickman (11)
Caldecote Primary School

Red

Red is hot
Red is blood
Red is danger
Red is your heart
Red is my team's kit
Red is when the sun comes down in the night
Red is smart
Red is my party
Red is crazy.

Robert Sheehan (9)
Cherry Hinton Junior School

Autumn

Autumn is red, yellow and brown
Autumn is the colour of a king's crown.
The colour of a flaming fire
The colour of beauty all around.
Autumn is the colour of a cup of cocoa
The colour of warmth.

Autumn has pleasant sounds
Like fallen leaves underneath your feet
The smell of fireworks in the air.
Autumn has a feel of freshness
Starting to get cold like frost.
Autumn has a tingling feel of warmth.

Like you're in a palace of fire and sun.
You feel like you're in a numb fire
A blinding sun with no burning light.
Sure enough you need a coat
Otherwise you'd feel like a mountain
Full of snow.

Autumn has more than an annoying wind
It has a wonderful colour.
Flaming red sunset instead of golden
Making the evening brighter with red.
Reminding you of how beautiful autumn is
Making the evening blend with colour.

In the morning it's like the first day
With a bright golden sunrise.
It shines through your window with
A wake up call 'Wake up, today is autumn'
So up you get to a palace of fire and sun
That's how it is until winter.

Kelly Rogers (8)
Cherry Hinton Junior School

THE COLOUR BLUE

Blue is the colour of the sea,
Blue is a colour of the rainbow,
Blue is the colour of the sky
And the wind.
Blue is the pencil case,
Blue is a car.

Blue is a wall,
Blue is the T-shirt,
Blue is the box.

And blue is the whole wide world.

Philip Mullen (8)
Cherry Hinton Junior School

The Rainbow Poem

Red is for red hot, the fire in your house,
Orange is for rainbow, sunset sun,
Yellow is the sun, a felt tip,
Green is the grass, a book bag,
Blue is my school uniform,
Indigo is the sky,
A violet hair bobble.

Hannah McCluskey (9)
Cherry Hinton Junior School

PREDATOR OF THE DEEP

The waters of the deep are silent,
The waters of the deep are still,
But at night it's different when the predator comes out
It's when you hear a scream and a shout!
The water turns red with blood,
The predator has had its meal,
So it settles down for another night,
Until again it has seal.

Zoe Farr (9)
Cherry Hinton Junior School

Voyage To The Sun

A ship of gold with an army of four
A ghostly ship with a silver door,
For it goes sailing in a lonely sky,
On the first day of December.

A lonely world, my life is so bad,
For it's got to be that I am so mad
Because nobody could survive,
The golden terror, the sun.

30,000 pieces of cheese, 2 bottles of pepper,
Which makes people sneeze,
100 pounds will never last,
The everlasting journey to the sun.

At last the journey comes to an end,
The messy sun and Cornhill bend,
It's no better than the word below,
So it's all a waste of time.
Well, alas peril
The journey's done
I'm baking hot because of the sun,
The one to ever survive but
It's all a waste for nothing at all.

Luke Mitchell (8)
Cherry Hinton Junior School

CHEETAH

Cheetah hanging on the tree,
Cheetah looking for his prey,
He sees it, he pounces,
Poor zebra, life is no more.
Cheetah walking around to see prey,
He spots it,
He lowers down,
Pounces and runs,
No more python.

Nick Hall (9)
Cherry Hinton Junior School

BLUE IS . . .

Blue is the ocean wide
Blue is great
Blue is a colour
Blue is a pencil case
Blue is the school uniform
Best of all, blue
Is the colour of the world.

Jordy Gent (8)
Cherry Hinton Junior School

MYSELF

S trong and confident,
T alks at school,
E ats burgers,
P roud person,
H as fun,
E njoys football,
N ice!

H ot babe,
A rtist,
R eads at school,
T edious!

Stephen Hart (8)
Cherry Hinton Junior School

My Sweet Little Puppy

Here's a sweet puppy who looks very sweet,
He's cuddly and furry and likes to eat.
He always gets muddy and has a bath.
But that doesn't mean he's on a raft.
His ears are floppy and his nose is round.
His feet are big and they're stuck on the ground.
But everywhere he goes his tail is waving to and fro.
His paws and his nails are sharp.
He sleeps in a bed, all cosy and warm.

Stephanie Taylor (9)
Cherry Hinton Junior School

MONKEYS

Monkeys large, monkeys small
Monkeys eating bananas
On furry branches, they play
Naughty monkeys nicking fruit
Kind caring mother monkeys
Rocking their babies to sleep
Exciting mother monkeys play on trees
Yellow bananas for monkeys' teas.

Swing on trees.

Jordan Keith (9)
Cherry Hinton Junior School

THE TREASURE I'LL ALWAYS PROTECT . . .

I am hiding a most precious treasure
It is so secret and so fragile
I must keep it safe
And guard it well
I cannot let you have it yet
I must not tell . . .

For now
It belongs only to me . . .

I must protect it
And keep it from harm
I am very tempted
To give you the key
But at times
I have wanted to throw it away

I need to be able to totally trust you
I want to let you in
But this treasure has become so tarnished
I don't know if I can let you in

It is so still . . .
So frightened of being exposed
It has been waiting for someone worthy
To appreciate
And delight in its beauty
And to take great care of it

Will you guard and protect it?
Will you be that special one?

Who will set my heart free?

Simone Johnson (9)
Cherry Hinton Junior School

SOUNDS BY THE SEA

Roar, roar, goes the wind,
Whoosh! Whoosh! Goes the sea,
Children scrambling across the sand,
To their mum and dad, snore, snore!
Mum and Dad are asleep!

Mums and dads buying ice cream
Children licking and saying 'Thank you.'
The sun is setting, getting late
Soon everyone has left.

Ruth Myers (9)
Cherry Hinton Junior School

A Hot Day

Hot and sweaty
need a drink and
some shade
get some ice cubes
get sunburnt
and a tan
boiling hot
red-hot
boiling hot
need something cold.

Hannah Bould (9)
Cherry Hinton Junior School

CHILDREN'S FEELINGS

Happy,
Crazy children
Shouting and
Screaming
About
All day
Long
Inside
And out!

Jemma Hubbard (8)
Cherry Hinton Junior School

ADULTS' NIGHT OUT

Happy
Jolly
Adults
Singing
About
Noisily
And
Silly
Dancing
In
The
Moonlight
Till
Dawn.

Roseanna Whitelegg (8)
Cherry Hinton Junior School

Snake

Snake slithers and slides through the desert
As quiet as a mouse
Snake as hot as a cooker at 200°
As light as a pillow
Snake a little bit faster than a tortoise
Snake as scaly as a crocodile
Teeth as sharp as an eagle's claw.

Matthew Beattie (9)
Cherry Hinton Junior School

FEELINGS

Sad
and
lonely
when
someone
dies

Happy
and
excited
when
it's

your
birthday,
mad
and
angry

when
someone
tells
you
off
and sometimes when it's your birthday
you *burst!*

Whitney Jackson (8)
Cherry Hinton Junior School

A POEM FOR A LOST BOOK!

Sad
upset
angry
gutted
silly
grumpy
done in
bored
in
a
rush
worried
annoyed
afraid
frightened
scared
upside down
sweaty
bright
dazed, shocked . . .
because it is right in front of me!

Elliott Unwin (8)
Cherry Hinton Junior School

AGES

When I was 1
I made a drum
When I was 2
I got some shoes
When I was 3
I broke my knee
When I was 4
I could open a door
When I was 5
I learnt how to dive
When I was 6
I ate Weetabix
When I was 7
I wished to be 11
When I was 8
I broke a plate
When I was 9
I drank some wine.

Oh yes, I'm ten!

Nicole Elbourne (8)
Cherry Hinton Junior School

SILLY ROMANS

Romans think they are so brave,
We're just going to send them home again.
Romans think to take rich London
We'll just show them.
Romans trying to invade,
But they can't beat the British rain.
Romans think they're having fun.
But maybe they should run.
Caesar calling his great force
They haven't got a single horse.
Romans coming again.
They still can't beat the British men.

Ben Whybrow (8)
Great Wilbraham Primary School

Horrible Romans

Romans are in an angry tone,
Always destroying our precious homes,
They invaded Planet Earth,
Ever since the place's birth,
They are also horrible teasers,
Led by their leader, Julius Caesar.

Adam Horsfield (7)
Great Wilbraham Primary School

Romans

Romans, Romans, they're a clever lot
They beat us once
They beat us again.

Gus Ramus (8)
Great Wilbraham Primary School

My Budgie

I once had a budgie, a budgie I once had
Until yesterday . . .
I went to feed him, but where had he gone?
I went to the cat and shouted at her
And this is what I shouted -
'Pussy cat, pussy cat, why are you licking your lips
With your whiskers so clean?
Pussy cat, pussy cat, where is my budgie?'

Sophie Warwick (8)
Great Wilbraham Primary School

Questions, Questions, Roman Questions

One day Rome might rule again,
Take over Britain and even Spain.

I wonder how Boudicca did die,
Was she poisoned or was that a lie?

Did Rome have no fear?
Did they chop off the British ear?

Romulus and Remus built Rome,
But did they invent the garden gnome?

But there is one question I need not ask,
To conquer the world is the Roman task.

Sean James Lynch (9)
Great Wilbraham Primary School

ROMANS

Romans think they're the best
I would like to rip their vest.

Romans, what a nasty lot,
I would like to stuff them in a box.

When the Romans are in bed,
Quickly, quickly, chop off their heads.

Joshy Wells (8)
Great Wilbraham Primary School

THE DUMB ROMANS

Romans are an extra silly lot,
When we kill them they will rot.
The main complaint you get from a Roman is:
They don't like the British wet,
Always dread the rain,
Wish they were back in Rome again.
When the Romans' wishes comes true,
They are at home too!

Julia Spindel (7)
Great Wilbraham Primary School

On The Way

Clang! Go the waves on the rocks
Clash! Went the wind in the night
Boom! When the boat hit the bay.

Freya Jackman (7)
Great Wilbraham Primary School

Roman Rule!

Augustus Caesar trotting on his horse,
Coming to kill the British force.

The Romans killed the British lot,
When Britain lost the brilliant plot!

Boudicca riding on her horse,
Running away from the Roman force.

Toby Frankau (9)
Great Wilbraham Primary School

The Silly Romans

Boudicca charging round and round,
In the next second, she's on the ground,
As flat as a pound!
Along comes a chariot running along,
Here comes the Tribune, 'Come along!'

Jenny Foreman (8)
Great Wilbraham Primary School

ROMANS AND ROME

Romans marching down the road
backpacks full of heavy load,

Romans hate the British rain,
wish they conquered Spain again,

Caesar yelling orders at them
while Boudicca's marching round the bend,

Boudicca lost but conquered many
paid so much she didn't have a penny,

Romulus built that city Rome
making it his very own home,

Boudicca drank that poisoned wine
drinking like a pig with swine.

Matthew Lawrance (8)
Great Wilbraham Primary School

THE STORM

The storm crashes, the storm bashes,
And waves wave, and Roman are scared,
But English are pleased, a storm came
and they won again.

Rebecca Mann (8)
Great Wilbraham Primary School

ROMANS

Here comes Caesar on his horse
Coming to fight the British force.
When he sees the British rain
He wishes he was in Rome again.
When Caesar saw the British men
He looked like a frightened hen.

Joseph Dean-Bryson (8)
Great Wilbraham Primary School

My Twin

My twin and I always have fun,
No one wants to play with us,
It's just me and my twin.
We play in the park and people stare,
We go swimming and I can hear muttering,
What's wrong with her?
I mean she's in my mind,
And she'll always be there for me.

Flossy Jones (10)
Park Street Primary School

Barbed Wire

Wire, doesn't spare flesh
Jabbed skin, jagged wire,
Metal, rushes to feed.
It lies there, looking innocent,
                    but it's not.
Wander by it, snatch!
You're caught in the trap.

Georgina Bowyer (10)
Park Street Primary School

The Dog

Max went out for his daily walk,
A chit-chat and a pleasant talk,
He'd left his human safe at home,
(His company, a garden gnome).

Our dear Max trudged into The Dog -
A pub ran by landlady Mog,
He wagged his tail and grabbed a beer,
And said 'It's very hot in here.'

'I know,' said Mog 'my paws are sore!'
Just then a dog burst through the door,
This dog's pub crawl was near the end,
To him the pub was his best friend.

'A whisky, babe,' the dog cried out,
'You've had enough, no need to shout!'
Said Mog and turned her head away,
At this the dog began to sway,

And wail and shout 'I wanna beer!'
Then Mog miaowed 'Get out of here.'
So up swooped Max to save our Mog -
He really was a gallant dog.

He showed the rascal to the door,
And barked 'Don't come here any more,'
Mog blushed and said 'Why thank you Max,
I think that now we can relax.'

Max said 'Ta, it is home for me,
My human needs his cup of tea,
I've left him back there all alone,
With no one but the garden gnome,

And he will need a little play,
Before we end another day.'

Hannah Wright (11)
Park Street Primary School

THE THINKER

There he sits
unmoving
and steady.
His eyes still,
and staring.
He will sit,
on the park bench,
thinking
for all eternity,
knowing
yet wondering.
He has lost
but
he has found
the knowledge,
the open door
to understanding.
And yet,
he'll be wandering
forever.

Rose Hughes (10)
Park Street Primary School

LESS REASON THAN NO REASON

Those, the sails of candyfloss,
And this the ship of tin
That take me through a cluttered place
Of fantasies, have been.

Through the Sea of Nothingness
And past the land of Oz,
Over the waves of tall brick walls
Because, because, because.

Under the sun of mouldy cheese,
And into the ocean of cream,
There she blows: the Wonderland
That Alice saw in a dream.

Out of the ship we clamber now,
And over the hills of Brie,
Through the fields of processed meat
And below the singing tree.

So floating there in the lake of clay,
Is Never Never Land
And there while looking at the sea
I'll stay young upon the sand!

Joe Minden (10)
Park Street Primary School

Obsession

Some people can't take their eyes off the box.
Some people love birds, nature and rocks.

Some people love games, athletics and sport.
Some people love drinking rum, whisky and port.

Can you stop a swot from going to school?
Can you stop a weight watcher from swimming
in a pool?

Are you obsessed?

Owen Taffinder (10)
Park Street Primary School

The Snake

He slithers quietly through the forest,
His skin is ugly and rough,
Other animals see him and scream,
Not to be harmful is his dream.

He sees his prey and strikes,
He kills it with a painful bite,
Then, he goes away in search of more,
And he'll be like that forever more.

Harkrishan Kaur (11)
Park Street Primary School

NOTHING BUT DEATH!

My journey to the hidden land,
Was tomorrow to begin,
I'd volunteered to give a hand,
Much to my chagrin.

I'm going on my journey now,
The crew are ready and set,
I've washed and scrubbed the wooden bow,
I cannot help but fret.

We sailed over the dancing seas,
Under the sky of blue,
Past the land of lush, green grass,
Past humming of striped bees.

A light flashed out ahead of us,
I said 'A storm has come,'
The crew were in a screaming rush,
There was no sign of sun.

Our journey had to end there,
The ship lay in the sea,
The waves ripped like a hungry bear,
The only survivor was me.

Jessica Halliley (10)
Park Street Primary School

My Family

I've got a sister who looks like a pig.
Wearing a wig while dancing a jig,
And likes to play
Almost all day.

I have a brother who looks like a monkey
And thinks he looks funky.
He likes to play on his bike
His name is Mike.

I've got a mum
Who says 'Life is fun,'
And likes to cook
She cares about her look.

I have a dad
Who is never sad
And likes to eat a cookie
While watching the footie.

I am called Anna
They say 'I'm a spanner.'
I love my family
And my best friend is Emily.

Emma Payne (9)
Park Street Primary School

CINEMA

Lights flickering,
People whispering,
Drinking Coke,
Chewing sweets and crunching popcorn.
Toddlers wriggling,
Seats flipping.
PGs, 12s, 15s too
Go to the cinema and see them all
Warner Brothers and Odeon
Cinema! Cinema! Cinema!

Scott Gyllenborg (11)
The Meadow CP School

TOFFEE

Round or square
Sticky brown toffee
Running slowly through my fingers
Slipping into my mouth
And through my body
Yum!

Then again.
Slipping through my fingers
Into my mouth
Down me
Faster and faster
Going in me
Down me
Yummmmm!

Faster and faster
Down me it goes
20 pieces
30 pieces
Lots and lots
Yum!

Where's my toffee?
All gone!

Kayleigh Salter (10)
The Meadow CP School

Chocolate Tin

I leave the chocolate tin out and hide.
Then you hear little footsteps.
There is Adam
He grabs four chocolate bars and
I go boo!
He goes running, his rubbery fat legs woooing
Off I go and Adam is still running
His rubbery fat legs going woo woo
And I am diving and jumping
Trying to catch him
And then he turns into a sort of hedgehog.
He tries to roll away.
I rip them away and he sits there crying
And me
Feeling generous
I give him a chocolate bar.

Christopher Kerby (10)
The Meadow CP School

My Dad's Dungeon

My dad's dungeon
he keeps me in there
if I don't do my room
or the washing up.
I don't like being in there
because it's full of spiders
and old packets of chips
and if I try and escape
I have to stay in there
for two whole days
and not a minute less.

Edward Malins (10)
The Meadow CP School

My Dream

I had a dream of a dog I might like
He was big and strong and his name was Spike
I never once heard him bark
Except when he chased the mail man around the park.

Although he is big and has a gruff bark
He is a real softie with eyes so dark
When we go to the park alone
He does not like to take a bone.

He does not like to take a stick
Although he is mighty quick
He does not like to run around
In fact he lies flat out on the ground.

Abby Henderson (11)
The Meadow CP School

MY FAVOURITE IS A TEDDY BEAR BUT HE ONLY WEARS HIS UNDERWEAR

Toys, I've got millions
Some people say I've got zillions
My favourite is a teddy bear
but he only wears his underwear
He is dark brown
his name is Clown
So toys, I've got millions
Some people say I've got zillions

Toys, I've got millions
Some people say I've got zillions
I've got over ninety
My second favourite's Bounty
I keep them on a shelf
I've got a monkey Elf
he had a big hole
so I fed him to a mole
So toys, I've got millions
Some people say I've got zillions

Toys, I've got millions
Some people say I've got zillions
My favourite's a teddy bear
who only wears his underwear
My second is called Bounty
his twin's called Mounty
My worst is Elf
who sits on a shelf
he had a big hole
so I fed him to a mole
Toys, I've got millions
Some people say I've got zillions

Emma Jopling (11)
The Meadow CP School

The Spot

The spot that lies upon my chin
Is big and red and very grim
'Ahh, it's a monster'
I shout to my mum
It's going to explode.
Now I look ugly,
Ugly as sin.

Rachel Burnett (11)
The Meadow CP School

FOOTBALL

Football, football, such a lark,
I play it in the garden, I play it in the park,
Running down the wing, and crossing it in
And my mate in the box shouting, 'On me head son.'

Football, football, such a lark,
I play it in the garden, I play it in the park
Bang, there goes a shot, screaming through the air,
Will the goalie save it, as he's standing there?

Football, football, such a lark
I play it in the garden, I play it in the park.

Matthew Caller (11)
The Meadow CP School

PRETENDING

Sometimes I pretend I'm a bird,
high in the sky,
flapping my wings,
in the summer sun,
I get a perfect view of everything underneath me.

Sometimes I pretend I'm an ant
with feet so tiny,
beetles, worms, and other nasty things are giants to me.
So I plod along feeling so small,
And don't get a perfect view of
anything at all.

Sometimes I pretend I'm a ship
blowing out steam from my chimneys
Sometimes I lie in bed and think,
I wonder what it would be like
to be one of these things?

Sonia Griggs (11)
The Meadow CP School

THE THING I LIKE TO DO

The thing that I like most to do,
is barge through people at rugby
but sometimes it isn't very cool
because I can get barged too.

The best days I love the most
is playing the very hard teams.
Though when I'm lying in the dirt,
they kick and stomp, and boy it hurts.

Harry Robbins (11)
The Meadow CP School

Wardrobes

Wardrobes sometimes scare me,
They open their huge, great mouths,
And suck in all the clothes,
And shut their mouths with a creak.

Wardrobes sometimes scare me,
Especially when you find,
Spiders and huge bits of fluff,
All over my nice, clean clothes.

Wardrobes sometimes scare me,
They stand tall in the night,
Creating shadows on the walls,
Wardrobes sometimes scare me.

Alice Newton (10)
The Meadow CP School

CYPRUS

I went to Cyprus on holiday
It was very hot and it did not rain.
I stayed in a hotel
Hotel Rose was its name.
I went swimming in the sea,
I jumped off a rock and hit my knee,
We went down to the town,
There were lots of things to see
And my mum brought a new coat for me.
My holiday was loads of fun,
Lazing about in the sun.

Alastair Page (11)
The Meadow CP School

SPIDERS

Spiders scuttling all around
lurking here and there
dark and long
and hairy things
predators of the night.

Spiders are ugly creatures
hungry for their prey
scheming through a hole
the predators of the night.

Alex Meddle (11)
The Meadow CP School

BIG SISTERS

Big sisters
They are monsters
Trust me, they are.

You can hear them coming a mile away
All you can think is,
Quick, run, before she says,
'I'm gonna getcha.'

You run
You run as fast as you can
You hide behind pillows
You scream and squeal
'Mum, Dad, help!'
But before you know it, she's got you.

You're in pain, no agony
But all you can do is lie there,
Trying to breathe
'How can I breathe,' you say
'When I have a 100-stone elephant sitting on me?'

You wait until she has gone
Then you run
Faster than you ever have before,
You run to your mum
Until you finally hear a
'Get to your room . . . now!'

Now you are safe,
Well, until the monster is released again.

Jessica Debnam (11)
The Meadow CP School

School

School, school, boring and sad
I hate, I hate school
Maths, English and history
I carry a bag as big as a bus,
I hate, I hate school.
PE in the afternoon
Mondays and Wednesdays
Playtime is a time to have fun,
I hate, I hate school.
Homework every night,
Oh I wish I could escape.

Gemma Cubbitt (10)
The Meadow CP School

Summer Holidays

I love summer holidays!
Lots of chocolate and melting ice cream,
Fun sports and games to play,
Off school for six whole weeks.
It's bliss!
Away from all the hard work
And boring teachers going on and on.
But the worst thing about the summer holidays is . . .
The bully at number 19.
He's mean and moody.
He beats me up.
In fact -
I hate summer holidays!

Josh Fay (11)
The Meadow CP School

My Holiday

My holiday is always the same,
Pack the car,
Get in the car,
Drive off,
Get to the port,
Through the port,
Round, round the corner,
Onto the ferry for nine hours,
Off the ferry,
Drive to the cottage.
Guess where we're going
France.

Rebecca Davies (10)
The Meadow CP School

TEACHERS

We mustn't put spiders,
In our teacher's jam.
She threatens us with the thought of ringing our parents
Or just in case we accidentally
Play a nasty trick.
Such as stealing all her chocolate
She would shut us in the cupboard.
Our other teacher:
When we go and see the teacher,
The best teacher of all,
She gives us sweets for anything
Like asking for a pen.
And never does she shout at us,
Or go charging round the room
Whenever we do our work
A tiny little bit wrong.
And the last teacher:
She gets put in the middle of this
Because she's not the best or worst.
And for me,
The best teacher would be none at all,
Just to be by myself.

Emily Brown (11)
The Meadow CP School

Hot Chocolate Croissants

My family and I stayed in France.
Down the lane there was a bread shop
white bread, dark bread, cakes and drinks
and best of all hot chocolate croissants,
so every morning I woke up
got dressed and walked down the hill
under the electric fence
and across the road
and down to the village of Chatel,
Chatel with its market every Wednesday
and all the skiing shops
and there it is -
the bread shop,
so there I am at the counter
speaking my best French
and lucky for me I manage to buy
four hot chocolate croissants and two long sticks of bread
I walk across the road
up the hill
under the electric fence
and back up to our flat
finally I'm on the balcony
the sun blazing down,
here comes my sister
and she says
'So where's my bread?'

Rebecca Jopling (11)
The Meadow CP School

My Friend Emily

My friend Emily is a very nice lass
My friend Emily is good at maths
My friend Emily is the oldest of five
My friend Emily is very alive

My friend Emily watches Casualty and Holby City
My friend Emily is very witty
My friend Emily is very daring
My friend Emily is also caring

My friend Emily is very tall
She also likes netball
My friend Emily has short hair
Emily and I are always a pair

My friend Emily wears a skirt
Surely she does not play in the dirt
My friend Emily hasn't got measles
She can't drive so she doesn't buy diesel.

Kate Allan (11)
The Meadow CP School

The Dome

The Dome was a waste of money
It was no fun at all.
And what were they thinking
When they built the wall?
They made it out of Kevlar
Why? I ask myself
It's not going to be shot
Well I wish it would be!
Some people say it's a breakfast bowl
Turned upside down.
It probably was the designer's fault
While he was having his breakfast
He must have drawn it upside down.

Jon Caller (11)
The Meadow CP School

TWO SIDES OF EVERY STORY

She walks down the street.
Her golden hair hangs loose.
People stop and stare.
Her clothes are wacky.
She is such an individual.
Her heels go clack-clack-clack on the cracked tiles.

But the strange thing is
She is not so brave
When it comes to school assemblies,
Or being the lead in a play.
She gets very scared,
Or chickens out.
So the big, cool gal
Is not so great
When it comes to presenting,
Or having a debate.

Imogen Haywood (11)
The Meadow CP School

My Annoying Little Devil

My brother is a little devil.
He's got a shaven head.
He looks like something out of Star Trek.
He's annoying,
And he moans a lot.
I see him every weekend
And he likes playing on the computer with me.
He never ever will be quiet
Even when he's asleep.
He snores and he doesn't leave me alone.
He doesn't let me sleep.
Day in, day out
He doesn't let me sleep.
But to annoy him
I pretend to sleep.
He falls asleep
So I'm asleep
Two hours later . . .
Aaaaahhhhh!
He's awake
My annoying little brother.

Craig Joyce (11)
The Meadow CP School

My Little Sister

I've got a little sister,
I hate her! I really do!
She pulls my hair,
And screams and shouts too.

I've got a little sister,
I hate her, I really do,
She rips up my pictures
And hurts me too.

Have you got a little sister?
You hate her, do you?
I bet she wears frilly dresses,
And looks like an angel too,
But she's a devil through and through.

Isabel O'Reilly (10)
The Meadow CP School

Falconry

The bird's talons
Pluck the glove
Like a nail hitting a lump of wood.
Its beaming eyes covered
With a leather hood.
It grasps its prey
With exceptional power,
And eats its food
In a quarter of an hour.

Sam Fall (10)
The Meadow CP School

LANDSLIDE

The muddy oak tree was sliding
down the grassy hill
It was raining buckets of mud
The green dragon was coming
Alone, not knowing what lay ahead.

Thomas Holah (10)
The Meadow CP School

The Match

The ball got kicked,
The players got picked,
I passed the ball
To someone tall.
He had a shot,
Harder than the lot,
It was a goal,
And then it snowed.
I was so glad
And they were mad.
We were winning.
Whistle dinging.

Rosie Softley
The Meadow CP School

SPACE

Space is a marvellous place
There's a Milky Way in space.
The Milky Way is a chocolate bar
But out in space is a bunch of stars
There is no gravity in space,
If you try and race,
There's no doubt about it, you'll
Just lose your pace.

Emma Burnett (9)
The Meadow CP School

THE PETS I HATE

The pets I hate,
Are next door to me.
They bark and growl at everyone.
Dogs they are.
One is tall, one is small,
One is fat, one is thin.
When they go for a walk they wear a hat,
It looks ridiculous.
Their owners are nice to me,
Their son is the paper boy,
He gives us the paper *sometimes.*
They like their dogs, their children do.
My dog hates the neighbour's dogs,
They bark at him and he runs off.
Every time we go near them
They bark and growl.
I hate those dogs, I really do.

James Gyllenborg (9)
The Meadow CP School

The Football Match

The match kicks off to a start
The players, hot and nervous
Everyone's running all over the place
No one trying to show their face
The team gets lots of service
Everyone's taking part.

The crowd are roaring and cheering
The players show off their skill
I sink into my comfy seat
Here comes the cross
'Score!' shouts the boss
So close to a goal
That must be Joe Cole
I get the ball, shoot and score
The game's over
It's a draw.

Matt Ashcroft (9)
The Meadow CP School

THE SEA

The sea, the sea, the sea
How big could it be?
Is it wide and filled with pride
Or is it long and very strong
Or is it thin and weak within
Or is it short like a second thought?
Nobody knows what it is
Or what it used to be.

Andrew William Hase (10)
The Meadow CP School

Living With Disability

The hearts were panting:
The breaks were breaking.

To the world of sadness,
The few days have gone by,
But she still sings that lullaby,
In that little sad warm heart of hers.

The hearts were panting,
The breaks were breaking,
To the world of sadness,
Her heart will desire, she does not fear
The scary memory of her days,
Though she did have some merry days,
She did play and play in her lonesome childhood.

The hearts were panting,
The breaks were breaking,
To the world of sadness,
She was brave, she was strong to live her day,
That she was wrong to be accused,
She used her hands to save a child,
For that she was the angel of the Lord.

The hearts were panting,
The breaks were breaking,
To the world of sadness,
But she still sings her lullaby,
In her heart she sings out loud,
For she can get her childhood back,
In her own little world.

Edward Allen (9)
The Meadow CP School

FEELINGS:

Feelings are: anger, excitement, happiness,
Fright, frustration, sadness and unhappiness
Frustration is controlled anger, like
losing games and races.
Excitement: record-breaking at very fast paces
and going on TV with a golden mic.
Unhappiness is bullying, getting kicked and hit
Punched and whacked by a football kit.
So that goes to show
How feelings know
To turn from bad to good.

Matthew Farmer (9)
The Meadow CP School

GREYHOUNDS

Greyhounds are fast, slim and slick
As fast as a lightning flick,
After a day of chasing the hare,
They cuddle up like a teddy bear
Soft as silk, a drink of milk
Soon curled up by the fire
As the years go by they get tired.

Brioni Rock (10)
The Meadow CP School

DONE SOMETHING WRONG

Done something wrong
But I can't see
Be myself
I must be me
Look around you
What do you see?
See the world
See me.

The guilty look
It comes from me
Tell the truth
Cos I can't see
I know I am
Not being me
Look around
See me

Now I've been told
I know I see
Very wrong
It's just not me
I'll make it up
Because I see
Nothing wrong
Now, he!

Julia Chesher (9)
The Meadow CP School

THE CHASE

The kidnapper's vicious smile.
The kidnapper with his thick, grey hair.
Like a chick or bear.
I turned. I saw the rain on the floor.
I saw something on the ground.
Something that I found.
We ran, ran down there for a while.
It was so unfair.
Speeding down the alley like a small hare.

Joe Donoughue (9)
The Meadow CP School

WAR

Guns up; guns down,
Guns shooting all around.
Bodies lie scrunched up.
Bombs hit, don't give up.
'Get up, don't let go,
Hold on until the end.
Give it that go, be strong.'
There's nothing wrong.
That's it, nearly there, up you get
Get out there.

Michelle Pelling (9)
The Meadow CP School

THE THINGS I ENJOY

I enjoy something yummy for my tummy
Like pizza, chips and salmon fishcakes from my mummy.

I enjoy diving to the bottom of the sea so peacefully
To see sea dolphins that swim so gracefully.

I enjoy new things, something different for me to do
Like cooking steak so new.

I enjoy helping someone, it's so cool
Some people think I'm a fool.

Nena Adrienne (9)
The Meadow CP School

HOLIDAYS

I like to go on holiday,
I like the sun and sea,
I like to go on holiday,
To see you and see me.
I like the thought of sun and snow,
And to look at mountains low,
I like to go sledging on all the mountains low.
I like to see the popping of the fireworks on fire.
I like the way we get there,
I like the way we fly,
Up the mountain,
Down the mountain,
Up in the sky.

Alli Nicol (9)
The Meadow CP School

PRISON

The questions here
His mind wasn't clear
He felt so stupid
For doing this crime.

The crime he committed
Was not even insisted
From the men he worked with
Now he's in his cell.

The guard is coming
With someone behind him
He thought it was his wife
But inside he was in strife
It wasn't his wife
It was the sergeant.

He's done lots of crimes
In his time
The crime done before he was caught
Was robbery.

The sergeant had ordered him to die
By being shot the next morning
He had just found out.

The night was long, he couldn't sleep
He knew his life was going to end
At twelve o'clock the next morning.
He woke the next morning
At ten o'clock.

Two hours later
He stood against the wall.

Joseph Antony Edwards (10)
The Meadow CP School

RAIN

Rain, rain, rain, again
Splashing on the windowpane
The sky rumbling, I sit in fear
To the great above we are only mere.

Its great shadow it does impose
Rays of sorrow it does enclose
Down to earth it falls
A great rumble he does call.

Amanda Biscombe (10)
The Meadow CP School

THE APOLLO 13

The crew of the ship
That had a snip of the mission,
The explosion that crippled the Odyssey
Meant the oxygen was lost.

The crew survived
Although it was dim they survived.
Their lives were spared by everyone who cared.

The electric came back on,
But it was cold
Still, they stayed bold.

They touched down in the Odyssey
To tell the story.

Ed Anderson (10)
The Meadow CP School

The Young Member Of The Family

When I leave for school
I feel sadness coming on.
As she waves goodbye
On the bus as I pass by.
When it comes to home time
I can't wait to see her.
I get in as she calls to me
I'm so glad to see her.
When it comes to love
You just can't stop
Loving your sister as time goes by
As you watch her grow like a butterfly.

Natalie Boreham (10)
The Meadow CP School

We're Winning

The kick-off's near,
The team sheet's clear,
We set foot on the pitch,
All pride in our blood,
A glint in our eye,
We'll slice through them like mud.

Ball's on the spot
We sweat from hot,
Then they start the game.
We're off like gunfire
Still a glint in our eye,
Going to cut them pie.

I take the ball,
I cross to the middle,
He controls in flight
As he shoots with great power,
Goalie jumps with great might,
But he's too late,
        we're winning . . .

Will Young (9)
The Meadow CP School